PANZERWAFFE AT WAR

(2) MOSCOW TO BERLIN

Robert Michulec & Thomas Anderson

THE MILITARY BOOK CLUB

603-609 Castle Peak Road
Kong Nam Industrial Building
10/F, B1, Tsuen Wan
New Territories, Hong Kong

printed in Hong Kong

The year 1941 was the third bad year in succession for the anti-Hitler coalition. German troops had conquered wide parts of Europe: Poland, Norway, Denmark and France were defeated and occupied. England got off cheaply after the Battle of Britain in that the country itself remained unharmed. The Allied troops in North Africa, however, were on the retreat. The autumn of 1941 put a question to the West: Would the Soviet Union be able to withstand the impetus of Germany´s battle-proven armored force, the *Panzerwaffe*? The tanks, the men inside, and, finally, the tactics seemingly swept away the forces of the world's largest country. Vast areas were invaded during the first month of Operation "Barbarossa", tens of thousands of armored vehicles were destroyed, and millions of Soviet soldiers were captured or killed in combat.

Hitler´s war plans projected that the collapse of the Soviet forces would occur in late autumn. However, despite enormous success, the German Army was not able to take Moscow. In December, a new ally joined the Soviet lines — 'General Frost'. Stuck in frozen mud, immobilized by masses of snow, severely injured or killed by temperatures below -40 ° C, men and weapons of the German war machine came to a halt.

1942 - Another successful year?

The End of "Barbarossa"

While the Germans faced this unpleasant situation, the Soviets launched a major counteroffensive. In order to hold the capital, the 10th Army attacked the German lines in the middle sector and encircled the 216th Infantry Division. The 22nd Army followed and penetrated the front between the German *Heeresgruppe Mitte* and *Nord* (Army Groups Centre and North). The Russians were able to take back more than 50 cities. The winter war showed one fact quite clearly: the Germans did not reckon with the problems the Russian winter would bring. The individual troops had to face the limits of their machinery. For example, the Maybach engines would not start in the cold and the relatively narrow tracks of the German tanks proved to be inadequate for deep snow. The tank formations were immobilized and defense was limited to holding trenches or strongpoints. The entire supply system collapsed since only inadequate transportation was possible. The *Panzerdivisionen* suffered a lack of fuel, ammunition, spare parts and food supply. The single soldier did not have any winter clothing or warm boots. In this situation, many of them died of exposure to cold, and the number of wounded increased dramatically. Subsequently, morale ran low, while the Soviets brought fresh troops from Siberia, men who were used to the cold. Still, the Germans were able to hold the lines, but with considerable losses.

Beginning in March and April, further offensive operations were planned. In May three Soviet Army corps would be destroyed at the Crimean front, and Sevastopol would be taken in July. Three further armies followed two weeks later, when the Soviet attempt to take back Kharkov failed. The German summer offensive was launched in late June 1942. The prime military objective now was the access to the Caucasian oil fields.

Until July the Germans held a straight line running from Leningrad over Moscow to Rostov on the Don. In order to take Stalingrad, *6.Armee* started an offensive in mid-August. The Soviet defenders were pushed back. However, progress of the attack was slow, and important objectives could not be taken. The real battle for Stalingrad started in September, when the suburbs were reached. Fighting was house-to-house, and personnel losses were high at both sides. On the 19th of September, five Soviet armies launched a large offensive from the River Don pointing to Stalingrad. One day later two further armies headed north. On the 22nd, both army groups met at Kalatsh, and the *6.Armee*, with more than 250,000 men, was encircled. The *4.Panzerarmee* tried in vain to relieve Gen. Paulus's men. Some days later Hitler ordered that the city had to be held at any price, a breakout being strictly forbidden. This was the death sentence for about 135,000 soldiers. Paulus, with some 90,000 men, now faced the war in captivity.

The Year 1942 in North Africa

Due to insufficient supplies, Rommel's troops faced a defeat at Sollum at the beginning of 1942 where the Afrika Korps lost some 13,000 men. Subsequently, heavy bombing raids were ordered on Malta, resulting in larger supplies for the German troops, which soon were fit for combat again. Three weeks later, Rommel was on the advance, and on the 21st of January the British 8th Army was pushed back. Surprised by this success, the British had to abandon Benghazi and Derna. In May the raid on Tobruk started, and the North African town fell in June. The impetus of the German advance forced the British back. Near El Alamein a new defense line was established. The first attack on this city failed, so strong was the British resistance. Because losses in July were very high, Rommel had to stop his advance again. The Germans were handicapped by inadequate fuel supply and were thus forced to dig in near Alam Halfa. Despite heavy fighting, the line was held. Before Rommel's troops could launch a second advance, Montgomery ordered a counterattack to break through the German lines. The fighting lasted for two weeks. At the beginning of November, two German fuel tankers were destroyed in the harbor of Tobruk, putting the Axis troops in an even more dangerous position. Faced with this situation, Rommel ordered a retreat, despite

Hitler's strict directions. Although the supply situation was always critical, Rommel was able to hold his lines.

In November, the Allies launched Operation "Torch", during which Morocco and Algeria saw large-scale landing operations. While Rommel was on the retreat, these troops prepared an attack from the west. It is interesting that the German *Generalfeldmarschall* was still able to retreat in an orderly fashion, with only 40 tanks in his inventory at the end of 1942.

The success of the *Panzers*

The comparison of German and Soviet tank production in 1942, giving special consideration to their combat value, is interesting. The most important development on the German side was the introduction of the long-barrelled 7.5cm KwK 40, which offfered a slight advantage over the Soviet 7.62cm tank gun. Beginning in March 1942, the Pz.Kpfw. IV Ausf. F2 was produced with this potent weapon. The successful assault gun units received this gun also, thus improving the tank force considerably. The Pz.Kpfw. III was improved as well, with the 5cm L/60 being introduced almost simultaneously in late 1941. Up until the end of that year, 877 Pz.Kpfw. IVs and 330 StuG IIIs armed with the 7.5cm L/43 guns, and other 365 StuG IIIs armed with the longer L/48, were issued to the tank troops. Some 1,907 of the Pz.Kpfw. IIIs armed with the 5cm L/60 were produced. Summing up, the German tank industry could field 3,560 tanks in 1942, tanks which were able to deal with the Russian KV and T-34 tanks. During this period the Soviet Union was able to produce 12,500 T-34 and 2,500 KV tanks.

The *Panzerwaffe* learned the following lessons:

1. Introduction of the long-barrelled 7.5cm L/43 guns, and to a smaller degree the less powerful 5cm L/60, shifted the balance of weaponry to the German side. Both the T-34 and the KV heavy tanks could be defeated successfully. In the North African theatre these weapons were introduced in lower numbers, but their performances impressed the Allies very much, resulting in the designations "Mk III special" and "Mk.IV special".

2. In 1942 the armor protection of the above-mentioned tanks reached a maximum of 50mm at the tanks's front plates. This increase was necessary, given the performances of the famous 7.62cm gun, and it was only an expedient. A further increase to 80mm was aspired to.

3. The tactical skills of the German tank formations were on a very high level. The great successes of 1942 were gained to a large extent due to superior tank tactics.

4. War industry production was at a dangerously low level. Supplies of ammunition, food and spare parts were insufficient. This was especially evident during the winter of 1941/42. Logistics and supply lines were often overtaxed due to the impetus of the German advance.

1943 - The Turning Point

It is difficult to say which incident marked the turning point of the Eastern campaign — the fall of Stalingrad or the failed raid on Kursk. The fact is that in 1943 the Germans lost the strategical initiative and their tank divisions were forced onto the defensive.

At the beginning of the year the situation was strained. All attempts to relieve the 6th Army failed. The collapse of the Hungarian and Italian allies in the Don River area resulted in a wide gap. In the south, Kharkov, Rostov and Krasnodar were liberated by the Soviets. But with an immense effort, von Manstein was able to take back Kharkov in March. Before the muddy season could set in, the front lines were stabilized again.

The Fall of the Afrika Korps

In North Africa, the turn of the year 1942/43 saw a large-scale advance of Montgomery's 8th Army. The extensive landings in northwest Africa during Operation "Torch" persuaded Rommel to retreat, since his supply situation was at a critical stage again. Several defensive lines were penetrated by the British, and on the 23rd of January, Tripoli was taken. Due to his orderly retreat, Rommel reached safe positions near Mareth. So successful was his retreat that Montgomery was not able to follow him, his own supply lines being overstressed. In this critical situation Rommel decided to attack the foe in the west — the inexperienced US and French armies. The battle of Kasserine Pass was Rommel's last victory. Though the pass was soon abandoned, this battle had cost the Allies more than 10,000 lives compared to 2,000 Axis losses. In April the Mareth line was taken by Montgomery, and the remnants of the Afrika Korps were surrounded at Bizerte and Tunis. Facing heavy supply losses, and with the British 'aircraft carrier' Malta viable again, Rommel capitulated some weeks later.

Kursk - the Last Great Offensive

On the Eastern Front the situation was relatively quiet. But the successes of the Soviets in the southern part resulted in a wedge, which protruded into the German lines in the Kursk area. In order to rectify this situation and to shorten the front line, Operation "Zitadelle" (Citadel) was launched. Plans dictated that on the 3rd of May, large tank formations should move into the wedge from north and south, and should subsequently take Kursk. The momentum was favorable, and the German 4th and 9th Armies were remarkably well-equipped. Large numbers of tanks, among them the newly developed Tiger and Panther tanks, were concentrated. The preparations also saw action by the heavy tank hunter "Ferdinand", at 68 tons the heaviest armored vehicle in 1943. But since Hitler himself demanded that all available heavy tanks be sent to the line of departure, the target date of the offensive was shifted repeatedly. These delays gave the Soviets precious time to prepare. Extensive trench systems were established and mine fields combined with *Pak-Fronten* (antitank gun positions) were prepared. When on the 5th of July, two months later, Operation "Zitadelle" was launched, the momentum of surprise was lost. It is only idle speculation, but one may assume that this attack could have been successful if it had started earlier. The Soviet tank force was exhausted after heavy winter fighting, while the Germans were able to field modern, superior tanks in considerable numbers (though much smaller overall than the Soviet tank strength).

The German offensive began on the 5th of July with the deployment of some 2,000 tanks. The Soviets could field more than 5,000 tanks and 20,000 guns and rocket launchers. The number of mines reached the millions, which led to massive losses in the initial stage of the operation. While the northern attack came to a halt after some 10 km (6.5 miles), the southern raid was more successful. Von Manstein was able to break through the Soviet lines of defense, his troops covering more than 40 km (26 miles). On the 12th of July they reached a place called Prokhorovka. This tiny vilage would see the largest tank battle in history; several hundred tanks were involved in the fighting. German veterans remember that some tank battles were fought at distances under 100 m (109 yards). It is clear that even the massive armor protection of the Tiger tanks was not effective in such situations. After 15 hours of fierce fighting, Soviet reserves headed south to menace Orel, and the battle for Prokhorovka ended in a stalemate.

The decision to halt Operation "Zitadelle" resulted from an occurance at another place. On the 10th of July Allied forces landed in Sicily. Since Italy and the Balkan region were regarded as preeminent, 1.Panzerdivision was ordered to Greece. Also, German statistics state that between the 5th and 19th of July more than 4,800 Soviet tanks were destroyed (compared to 1,000 German losses). "Zitadelle" was a large-scale failure. Wrong decisions, the shifts of the attack date, insufficent supplies, the dogged resistance of the Soviet defenders, and the intervention of the Allied forces in Italy all influenced the turning point of WW II.

Now the Soviets took the initiative. In early August the Woronesh front was pierced, and the Germans had to abandon Belgorod and Kharkov. From August to December the Soviets launched a series of offensives between Smolensk and Rostov. While the Germans had to give up town for town, their retreat was very orderly, and they inflicted very heavy losses on the enemy.

The March to the Gustav Line

The landings in Sicily were relatively successful. The invasion was launched on the 10th of July, and a mere five weeks later Patton and Montgomery took Messina. Sicily was liberated. The British 8th Army crossed the Strait of Messina in early September, but this attack was only a feint meant to lead the German defenders south. However, Kesselring, the commanding *Generalfeldmarshall*, expected a large invasion in the Gulf of Salerno. He was indeed right, for on the 9th of September US troops were there. The German resistance was fierce, and only small bridgeheads could be taken and held at great loss. One week later the situation was cleared up when British reinforcements from the south reached the bridgeheads. The Germans retreated to their defensive line, the *Gustav-Linie*. The Allies reached these fortifications at the end of 1943.

1943 in Retrospect - The Situation of the *Panzers*

1943 was an important year for the *Panzerwaffe*. That is when the reorganization of the tank arsenal was started. Initiated by the revolutionary T-34 tank, new German tank developments reached the front. The heavy Tiger was intended for concentrated attacks to pierce the enemy lines, and the medium Panther would supersede the obsolete Pz.Kpfw. III and IV as the main battle tank. The following conclusions can be drawn:

1. The Tiger tank dominated the battlefield of 1943. Its armor was strong enough to withstand most enemy guns at most combat ranges, while its deadly 8.8cm gun was able to knock out any tank at distances well beyond 2,000 m (2,200 yards).

2. The Panther was lighter. Provided with sloped armor, it offered excellent protection, as well. The high performance 7.5cm L/70 gun achieved even better armor penetration than the Tiger's gun.

3. Although the performances of the Tiger and Panther sound very impressive, their tactical and strategical use was limited. Very high costs resulted in low production numbers, and the desired numbers could never be reached. Due to hasty introduction, the technical reliability was poor, and many tanks had to be abandoned due to minor damage. The excessive weight (56 and 46 tons, respectively) made recovery difficult and often impossible.

4. The combat value of the most important German tanks, the Pz.Kpfw. IV and StuG III, was increased by several measures. So, at the beginning of Operation "Zitadelle", most vehicles were armed with the powerful 7.5cm L/48 gun, and the frontal armor was reinforced to 80mm. Also, armor skirts were added to the sides for additional protection. Thus, these vehicles were able to deal with most Soviet tanks.

However, the main problem of the German tank force was the inadequate industrial capacity. The number of tanks available at the beginning of Kursk is interesting. Although the Germans were comparatively strong, the Soviets fielded about 2.5 times as many tanks as compared to Germany — 2,000 against 5,000. In North Africa, Rommel had some 500 tanks compared to 1,200 Allied vehicles. This disproportion would worsen until the end of the war, and in the long run it would decide the war.

1944 - Retreat on all Fronts

The situation on the Eastern Front again became critical in early 1944. In the southern section, Kirovograd was lost in January. By May the Soviets had advanced to Sevastopol, and the Crimea was taken back. The Polish border was dangerously threatened. Von Manstein, with his *Heeresgruppe Süd* (Army Group South), inflicted very heavy losses on the enemy, German tactical skills still being superior.

In Italy, the *Gustav-Linie* saw intensive Allied attacks. In February 1944 heavy fighting took place at Cassino. Two German counterattacks failed, but the enemy couldn't take this important objective because of the strong resistance. Finally, in May, after heavy air raids and artillery duels, Polish troops marched into Cassino. The successful destruction of German supply lines by fighter bombers was an important reason for the breakthrough of the Gustav Line.

In June 1944, the western Allies fulfilled an old Soviet demand and established a second front. Large US, British and Canadian forces landed on the Normandy coast of France. Despite German resistance, some bridgeheads could be held. The Germans hesitated for some days since Hitler expected the main landing to take place farther up the coast. When strong German forces were finally sent to France, the Allies already had left their bridgeheads. In mid-July Caen was taken. At the end of July, General Bradley's US 1st Army sallied forth at St. Lo. This was a decisive move, and after regrouping, the Allied forces pushed back the defenders.

In August Paris was liberated. Having reached the Seine River, the western Allies were uncertain how to proceed to Germany . . . and then to Berlin. Montgomery voted for a strong wedge to be driven into the industrial area of *Ruhrgebiet*, which would then turn east to fight its way to Berlin. Eisenhower, however, saw danger in this plan because the flanks of this force would be threatened by the highly motivated German Army. So, a slow advance over the entire front was favored. One strategical problem involved supplies, which had to be transported over a distance of some 500 km (310 miles). It was essential for the Allies to capture a port near the front. At the end of August Antwerp was liberated, thus solving the problem. From then on the advance was stable, and the German frontier was reached in mid-September.

In mid-1944 the situation on the Eastern Front became critical for the German defenders. The enemy concentrated large forces in the area of Army Group Centre. On the 20th of June, partisans destroyed the railway network at more than 10,000 places. Two days later the Soviets launched a heavy artillery strike, more than 380 barrels being concentrated per front kilometer. The counteroffensive pushed directly into the surprised German lines. The defence collapsed and the entire army group had to be withdrawn. In July, Minsk was lost, followed by Riga in the North and Brest Litovsk. The Russians soon reached the Polish border. The Germans were eager to defend Warsaw, though, and the remnants of *Heeresgruppe Mitte* were able to hold the town. One reason for this is that the Soviet supply lines possibly were overstrained since they had to cover more than 700 km (435 miles). Action at the front came to a halt for some time. This gave the Germans precious time to regroup their defenses and transport fresh forces to the east.

In the meantime, the Leningrad front moved west, pushing the Germans back to Riga and Kurland, where they were encircled. While Riga fell in mid-October, the Kurland pocket was defended until the end of the war.

In August, the Soviets attacked the German *Heeresgruppe Südukraine* (Army Group South Ukraine). Again, so strong was the attack that the German forces had to be withdrawn. Romania and Bulgaria surrendered in August/September.

The end of 1944 saw the German forces pushed back to the borders. In December, a last major offensive was begun. On the 16th, eight tank divisions headed north. The main military objective was the capture of Antwerp in order to destroy the Allied supply lines. The US troops were taken by surprise, and the mighty Allied air force was nailed to ground by bad weather. The initial success of the Ardennes offensive came to a halt after some days. The Allied resistance became stronger, the weather better. The bitter fighting resulted in a six-week delay for the western Allies, but it destroyed those German reserves that possibly could have beaten back the Soviet spring offensive.

Panzers in 1944 - Quantity beats Quality?

In 1944 the German *Panzers* lost their halo of invincibility almost completely. Pushed back on all fronts, their superiority became doubtful. The reasons were manifold:

1. Although the modern German tanks were still superior, the technical margin narrowed. The Soviet 85mm and 122mm, the British 17 pdr. and the US 90mm guns were able to deal with the armor of the Panther and the Tiger/E at most combat ranges. The Tiger/B remained a difficult opponent, but even this heavy tank could be overcome during combat.

2. The lessons of modern tank warfare were learned by all participants, and their tactical skills slowly but surely reached the German standards.

3. The vast numerical superiority of the Allies decided most tank vs. tank battles. Only in very isolated situations were German tank forces able to achieve local successes — small gains that were soon lost again.

4. Allied air superiority made German offensive planning impossible, and, even on the defensive, combined air and artillery assaults rapidly broke down any resistance. The losses of armored vehicles were extremely high at the Western Front. Lacking antiaircraft protection, the supply

lines also became targets for air raids.

1945 - War in Germany

By the beginning of 1945 the western Allies had reached the Rhine River in the north at Nijmegen and in the south at Strasbourg. The Ardennes offensive had blocked the advance in the center, where the river was not reached until March. Another German attempt to stop the US 7th Army, Operation "Nordwind", failed some days after it was launched. On the 7th of March, an intact bridge was taken at Remagen. This important objective allowed the further advance of US troops. Three weeks later the Rhine was crossed at four more places. With their command structure and their supply line for food and weapons having completely collapsed, the German troops retreated.

Advancing steadily, the Allies invaded the *Ruhrgebiet* industrial area, and British troops liberated the Netherlands and drove into northern Germany. The center of Germany was reached in April, and the way to Berlin was free. The wish of the war-weary German civilians, however, was not to be fullfilled. Because the western Allies' advance to the east stopped at a line leading from Lübeck in the north to Nuremberg in the south, the complete eastern part of Germany was left to the Soviets.

German resistance in the east was much more dogged than in the west. But, facing overwhelming Soviet military forces, the defense broke, and more and more land had to be abandoned. The attempt to relieve Budapest, where some 30,000 men were encircled, failed. On the 13th of January, a new offensive threatened the Germans in the northern regions. After five days of fierce fighting, East Prussia was cut off and the Baltic Sea was reached. Some days later Warsaw was taken. At the beginning of February, after a fast and bloody advance, the Soviets reached the Oder River. The German defensive positions were bypassed or, when necessary, neutralized. The victorious Soviets came to a halt at the banks of the Oder River. There all forces were concentrated for the deciding advance — the raid on Berlin.

With Budapest fallen, the Soviets headed to Vienna. Hitler ordered that the oil fields near Lake Balaton were to be held. Subsequently, 6.SS-Panzerkorps surprisingly attacked the enemy and was able to establish new defensive postions at the Danube River. Here the first combat of Infra Red-equipped German tanks is reported. Instead of gaining even minor successes, the German counterattack came to a halt on the 16th of March. Once again supply and fuel problems, as well as the vast superiority of the enemy, decided the fight. Vienna was taken on the 14th of April.

In this unenviable situation the Germans had only one army intact, Schörner's *Heeresgruppe Mitte*. Despite being trapped by the Soviets, these relatively strong forces held on to the last remaining German industrial facilities in Czechoslovakia. In April, Schörner tried to relieve the capital. Although this counterattack inflicted heavy losses on the Soviets, it was to fail in the end. However, Schörner held his last positions until the 11th of May.

The attack on Berlin was launched on the 20th of April, but a massive preparatory bombardment hit the Germans four days earlier. Statistically, the Soviets were able to concentrate an artillery density of one gun for every five meters (sixteen feet). The fighting on the Oder line was bloody; Berlin was to be held at any price. Due to their vast numerical superiority, the Soviets broke through quickly, and *9.Armee* was pocketed in Frankfurt/Oder. By the 25th of April Berlin was surrounded.

In the west, the *Ruhrgebiet* was lost, and the German troops there capitulated. Soon the cities of Munich and Hanover also fell. Only the troops in Berlin, Schörner's battle group and units in Kurland continued to resist. However, when Berlin was finally taken, the war in Europe ended.

Conclusion - *Panzerwaffe* in Retrospect

The success of Germany, a relatively small country, has always stunned historians and political scholars. Of course, the momentum of surprise favored the German aggressors in Poland at the beginning of hostilities in 1939. Also, the non-uniform position of the Western neighbors, France and England, supported Hitler, who was always able to hide his actual strength. Indeed, it is possible that he could have been stopped in this early stage of the war. The invasion of France was the second logical step since its own forces were relatively weak. The skill of the German soldiers, who were led into combat with superior tactics, including the massive employment of tanks in the best possible manner, would decide the early course of war. Even the initial stage of "Barbarossa" and the raid in North Africa in 1942 were successful, with the *Panzers* sweeping away any resistance. However, when Soviet tank production capabilities proved to be stronger than Germany's, the advance was stopped. With the United States's entry into the war, Germany's fate was sealed. The combined industrial power of the largest communist and capitalist countries decided the war. Still, it would take three more years of bloody fighting to finally win it!

The German *Panzers* proved superior in most situations, either due to a clear qualitative edge (Panther vs. M4) or due to the more skilled operation of this weapon (Pz.Kpfw. IV vs. T-34). However, this clear advantage in technology was relative in many situations. Inadequate supply, poor reliability in the field, and massive air strikes were other deciding factors in the tank battles of World War Two.

The Year 1942

Although obsolete, more than 500 Pz.Kpfw. 38(t) tanks were in service at the beginning of 1942. With their thin armor and 3.7cm gun, their combat value was very limited. So, from mid-1942 they were used primarily for reconnaissance and anti-partisan purposes. These Ausf. Gs are shown advancing in the northern sector of the Eastern Front near Leningrad.

Compared to most German tanks, the massive Russian KV-1 was an invincible foe. In many cases, only the *Heeresflak* with its 8.8cm Flak gun was able to handle this threat. This uparmored KV-1 Model 1941 was destroyed by *Heeresgruppe Mitte* in early 1942.

This column of Pz.Kpfw. III Ausf. Js (armed with the 5cm KwK L/42) is advancing to the Kharkov area in March 1942. Extra fuel drums are stowed on the engine deck, a common practice in the early stages of Operation "Barbarossa". The second battle for Kharkov was one of the finest examples of German armored warfare.

In the northern region, Finnish troops fought alongside the German tank force. Here Finnish infantrymen follow a Pz.Kpfw. II Ausf. C in the vast woods of Karelia. Here, where the rapid advance quickly turned into positional warfare, the light tanks performed better than in the large-scale tank battles of the middle or southern districts.

Autumn and spring in Russia brought new, unexpected troubles for the German troops. Mud — very deep and a problem even for tracked vehicles — stopped all movement. Here a Sturmgeschütz (StuG) III Ausf. E of StuG.Abt.226 tows a lorry (truck) through a mud hole. Veterans say that many tanks were ordered for the specific purpose of making supply possible.

Another StuG III Ausf. D of StuG.Abt.226 is being recovered by an 18-ton half-track. These massive Sd.Kfz. 9s were perfect recovery vehicles for vehicles of the 20-ton class. The tow cables are just visible between the vehicles as they maneuver through the snow-covered landscape.

This Pz.Kpfw. III Ausf. J (5cm KwK L/42) monitors a snowy road in Russia. In the background, a typical supply scene takes place. Lacking lorries, the *Wehrmacht* had to rely on horse-drawn wagons. The tank wears an interesting winter camouflage consisting of thin, irregular white stripes over a gray base. The turret number '634' is barely visible.

A Sd.Kfz. 252 ammunition carrier of StuG.Abt.226 waits for action. This highly specialized version of the versatile light armored personnel carriers (APC) performed quite well. Their armor protection allowed them to supply StuGs near the front lines.

A number of Pz.Kpfw. IIIs of different production lots gather in a Soviet town. The third vehicle appears to be brand-new since the camouflage on all the others has worn off. Though upgunned with the L/42 gun prior to "Barbarossa", these tanks became obsolete on the battlefields of 1942.

Judging by the production numbers, the Pz.Kpfw. III was the most important German tank of 1942/43. This Ausf. H was photographed as it waited in a column. The basic frontal armor of 30mm was reinforced to 50mm with welded steel plates. Additional protection was achieved by the attachment of large sections of spare tracks.

Two StuG III Ausf. Fs, followed by an ammo carrier, advance over muddy ground. The assault guns are fitted with large wooden crates on their engine decks. Their non-standard markings denote the platoon (recognizable by the bars' color) and the vehicle number. Identification markings like these were often seen in assault gun units, which very often fought independently.

A Pz.Kpfw. IV Ausf. D is being passed by a Pz.Kpfw 38(t). Many divisions still had a lot of these former Czech tanks in their light platoons. Uparmed with a long-barreled 7.5cm gun, the Pz.Kpfw. IV would serve as Germany's main battle tank until the war's end. This older version of the 7.5cm L/24 soon proved to be obsolete for dealing with the T-34 and KV-1.

This battle-proven StuG III Ausf. D carries a lot of extra equipment. This practice was neccessary because the assault guns were so cramped inside. Two wooden beams were stowed on the fenders for recovery purposes. Spare tracks, additional running wheels and Soviet towing ropes complete the load of equipment.

In early 1942 a new version of the StuG III appeared — the Ausf. F. This assault gun was provided with the 7.5cm StuK 40, a long-barrelled gun with high velocity. It was able to deal with any enemy tank. This interesting photo of an Ausf. F was retouched by the censors, who deleted the muzzle brake so that enemy intelligence would be misinformed.

In the late spring of 1942, the first Pz.Kpfw. IVs fitted with the high velocity gun seen here were delivered to the front-line units. This Ausf. G was able to deal with all Soviet and English tanks at distances up to 700 m (765 yards). The tank at right is finished in plain dark gray, with the turret number '431' being painted in white.

Suffering from the heavy fighting in Russia, many armored formations were transferred to occupied France for refitting. There, new equipment was supplied and fresh troops were integrated and trained. In this photo, APCs perform an assault on dug-in infantry who were expecting them. The half-tracks in the foreground are older Sd.Kfz. 251 Ausf. Bs, while the other is a more recent Ausf. C.

Somewhere in France a Pz.Kpfw. III Ausf. L passes a group of curious civilians. The tank's 5cm L/60 was a long-expected improvement, but it was still not the gun the *Panzertruppe* had waited for. Compared to Soviet tank guns and armor, it was cleary inferior.

Shortly after their arrival in France, these tanks of 26.Panzer-Division head out to conduct maneuvers. Compared to the conditions endured by the troops on the Eastern Front, the units stationed in France enjoyed the sunny side of life. Although an Allied landing was expected, nobody believed the threat was serious. However, the *Wacht am Kanal*, the guard at the Channel, was a boost for both regular and psychological warfare.

A platoon of APCs belonging to 10.Panzer-Division moves to the Mediterranean coast of France in November 1942. The leading vehicle is a Sd.Kfz. 250/3 command vehicle, while the others are standard APCs. Some weeks later, the division was transferred to Tunisia, where it was destroyed in early 1943.

The situation in North Africa was different than in Russia. Highly motivated troops were led by very capable officers. Although poorly equipped, the Germans were able to invade large areas. Here Major-General von Bismark stands on the turret of his Pz.Bef.Wg. III Ausf. H command tank. The gun was a dummy, thus saving space for the extended radio equipment.

Unusual brothers-in-arms. Here a Pz.Kpfw. IV Ausf. D stands beside a captured Matilda Mk.2. While the Matilda lacked firepower— it was equipped with a 2 pdr. gun (40mm), its German opponent's flaw was its poor armor protection (30mm at the nose).

Seen here in August 1942, a Pz.Kpfw. III Ausf. H is being unloaded in Benghazi. The vehicle is fitted with the short-barreled L/42 gun and an interesting basket at its rear, which was designed for carrying fuel cans over the vast terrain of North Africa. (Photo: Hasler)

An Ausf. L belonging to the same unit waits near the harbor of Benghazi for further orders. The vehicle seems to be finished in a desert sand paint scheme rather than in dark gray. Note that the Pz.Kpfw. III appears to be brand-new and shows no sign of damage. (Photo: Hasler)

Yet another version of the Pz.Kpfw. III, this one an Ausf. N armed with a 7.5cm L/24 gun, stands near a captured Humber armored car. The Afrika Korps used as much enemy materiel as possible. There were even situations when the inventory consisted more of captured tanks than German ones. (Photo: Hasler)

In this photo a 3-ton truck, which has been converted to a workshop, is employed to remove the engine cover of a damaged Pz.Kpfw. III Ausf. J. Apparently, the engine broke down, which was quite a frequent problem in the heat of North Africa. Note how the tank crew members escape the sun by sitting in the shade created by their vehicle.

A German cargo transport ship unloads a Pz.Kpfw. III Ausf. L. The long way to Africa was dangerous since Malta was not occupied by the Germans. Many ships were destroyed by air raids that succeeded in sinking valuable reinforcements for the *Deutsche Afrika Korps* (DAK). Having reached the ground, the Pz.Kpfw. III is loosed from the lifting belts. Several Tunisian harbor workers stand on top and around the vehicle. This view shows to advantage the extra fuel cans stored in the rack atop the rear of the tank.

Standing in his famous command vehicle called *Greif* (griffin), General Field Marshal Rommel discusses the fighting situation with DAK troopers. Although cramped inside, the Sd.Kfz. 250 was very popular in the command version. This photo was taken near Tobruk.

A German antiaircraft platoon, which is equipped with 2cm Flak 38 guns, passes a column of Italian tanks in the barren North African desert. The M13/40 tanks were no match for their British adversaries. The Kfz. 69 (Horch) is equipped with anti-flare covers over the windscreen.

Italian infantrymen wearing wet weather gear gather around a German Pz.Kpfw. II Ausf. F. Not uncommon weather in North Africa, an autumn rainstorm drenches soldiers and vehicles. The officer with the briefcase seems to take it all in stride, though.

Photographed in Tunis in December 1942, this Pz.Kpfw. IV Ausf. F2 is encircled by civilians. Armed with the powerful 7.5cm KwK L/42, this version was quickly called 'Mk. IV special' by the British. It was able to defeat any enemy tank at ranges of more than 1,000 m (1,093 yards). The tank is finished in sand yellow, and the turret number is probably red with white outlines. Extra equipment is carried on the fenders and turret. Of interest is the large antenna deflector fitted below the barrel.

On patrol in Russia, this Pz.Kpfw. III Ausf. J (L/42), which is loaded down with infantry, passes a Panzerbefehlswagen III Ausf. G command vehicle that is probably from the battalion staff section. The command tank was fitted with a dummy gun, its only armament consisting of an MG34 in a ball mount to the right of the dummy gun. Once again, a Soviet-style towing rope was pressed into service.

The railway line to Alexandria repeatedly was a reason for fighting. This destroyed medium tank was probably put out of service by 8.8cm guns. The derelict M3 Grant was the first Allied tank that could deal with the Mk. III and Mk. IV specials.

Approaching a burning Soviet village, this Pz.Kpfw. III Ausf. L monitors the road. The commander looks out of his hatch, very carefully, too, since head injuries were common with tankers. The L/60 gun gave the Pz.Kpfw. III a fair chance when meeting T-34 tanks.

Some more Pz.Kpfw. III (Ausf. L and M) tanks deploy across the vast Russian plains. Armored infantry in half-tracks can be seen supporting the advance. Again, a rack filled with extra equipment is visible on the engine deck of the tank at center. Its turret number is no doubt painted in red with a white outline.

Having reached the devastated enemy positions, the crew of this Pz.Kpfw. III Ausf. L has left the tank, probably to have a closer look at a damaged part on the rear of the hull. The vehicle displays a two-digit number painted in white on the turret sides.

Slowly moving along the Russian steppes, this Pz.Kpfw. IV seems to be an 7.5cm-armed version. The photo was retouched by German censors, who almost completely deleted the new L/43 gun barrel of this Ausf. F2. These vehicles were able to deal with all of the Soviet tanks under normal conditions. A white number '401' was applied to the sides of the turret.

A fine shot of a *Truppenluftschutzwagen*, a Kfz. 4 wheeled vehicle armed with twin MG34 machine guns. Note how the gunner zeroes in on the enemy planes through the antiaircraft gun sight extending above the gun barrels.

This scene shows a pair of Pz.Kpfw. IV Ausf. Gs being shipped on a ferry at Mariopol near Rostov. The large Black Sea was well suited for extensive naval operations, and, of course, this more modest means of transportation.

Here a StuG III Ausf. E of StuG.Abt.226 is being transferred over a river by bridge-building engineers. Four pontoons have been combined to carry a bridge section, thus creating a provisional ferry. Since the officers in the foreground seem quite unconcerned as they watch the activity, this was probably only an exercise.

With the autumn mud announcing the coming Russian winter, the crew members of this 3-ton truck await further orders. The load they carry consists of quite practical equipment — sledges and skis. The German Army was much better prepared for this winter than one year before. The truck, a Mercedes L 3000 S, wears a crude winter whitewash on a dark gray background.

The 2cm quadruple antiaircraft gun was one of the most feared weapons on the Eastern Front. Intended for action against low-flying dive bombers, it was often used to engage ground targets. The warmly dressed crew of this Sd.Kfz. 7/1 is seen on a cold November day as they prepare for the next action.

This StuG III Ausf. F of StuG.Abt.226 displays a perfect winter camouflage. A tarpaulin is used to cover the superstructure, which had many openings. The assault gun has been provided with winter tracks. Note that parts of the fenders are missing; battle damage like this was quite common. This early Ausf. F shows no additional armor at the bow.

In December 1942, StuG.Abt.226 received its first StuG III Ausf. Gs. These were of the very early production lot, showing a revised superstructure with steep angles at the front plates. Again the camouflage is perfect.

The twin machine guns that were often seen mounted to the *Truppenluftschutzwagen* (Kfz. 4) could be dismounted and used for static antiaircraft defense, as well. The soldier in this photo, who demonstrates the proper firing position, wears white winter camouflage over his uniform.

In late 1942 a number of Pz.Kpfw. IIIs were reworked to receive the 7.5cm L/24 gun. New ammunition provided this gun with better penetration data than the 5cm KwK. Most of these vehicles were despatched to Tiger units as direct support weapons. This vehicle was reworked from an Ausf. N.

The Year 1943

Seen in full action, this 8.8cm Flak fires at ground targets. The '88' was a much feared weapon, as much in the desert as in Russia. This gun has been thoroughly camouflaged by adding white stripes. The commander observes the target while a shell is blasted its way.

A StuG III seeks cover in a dugout position. The assault gun will soon disappear from enemy observers and be protected against the weather. Positions like this were very effective as a defensive tactic. This Ausf. G of an early production lot shows welded-on extra armor and side skirts. The muzzle brake and the superstructure are covered by tarpaulins.

The gun shield of the 8.8cm Flak gun shows an impressive score. Four artillery observers, 4 guns, 8 pillboxes, 27 tanks, and 10 enemy planes were destroyed either by this particular gun or by the battery (which seems more likely). The fact that the tanks are represented by an M3 Lee denotes that this Flak saw action in the southern sector of the Eastern Front.

A pair of Sd.Kfz. 231 armored cars are seen here during a funeral for two officers of 19.Panzer-Division. The photo is interesting since the vehicle at left is of an older production lot with extra armor plating (*Zerschellerplatte*) at the front. The armored car on the right, which is of a later lot, features alterations at hull, fenders, visors, and gun shield.

This Pz.Kpfw. III Ausf. N (reworked from Ausf. L), which is shown passing through a French city, is camouflaged in desert sand with brown blotches. The tanks belonging to this unit were soon transferred to North Africa. The Ausf. N was the final variant of the Panzer III.

Many armored units were sent to France for refitting. These armored cars of 7.Panzer-Division are late production Sd.Kfz. 232s sporting the 1.3m star antenna d instead of the prominent frame antennas. The vehicles are still finished in plain dark gray.

Taking a brief break from protecting a French harbor with an imposing quadruple-barelled antiaircraft gun, the crew of this Sd.Kfz. 7/1 enjoys their lunch in the Mediterranean sun. The dark gray half-track is towing an ammunition trailer.

This photo, taken sometime around the turn of the year 1942/43, shows the crew of a 5cm Pak 38 cleaning up their gun. The wires wrapped around the gun shield allow for the application of foliage. In the background is parked the towing vehicle, a brand-new Krupp Protze.

Somewhere in Italy the commander of a Sd.Kfz. 223 communication/recce armored car carefully watches the street fighting taking place in an Italian city. These old vehicles performed much better in the dry climate of southern Europe than under the rough conditions of the Eastern Front.

Here a dispatch rider mounted on a Zündapp motorcycle passes a burning T-34 Model 1943. The German dispatch rider system was very successful, so much so that the Soviets copied the system, even to the point of using motorbikes with a sidecar.

Shown during Operation "Zitadelle", a mixed tank column of 3.SS-Panzer-Division moves up to the front. The Pz.Kpfw. III to the right is an Ausf. L with interesting camouflage consisting of green blotches on a dark yellow base. In the background, Pz.Kpfw. IV Ausf. Gs or Hs are visible.

Most tank units taking part in Operation "Zitadelle" were made up of a mixture of tanks. The 3.SS-Panzer-Division 'Totenkopf' ('Death's Head') had Pz.Kpfw. IIIs and IVs in its inventory. Some of the tanks are fitted with side skirts, some are not. Note the three-bar marking on the turret skirt, again a temporary marking used during the Kursk campaign.

Tigers of 2.SS-Panzer-Division move up to the front during Operation "Zitadelle". With Tigers available in greater numbers, new tactics were introduced. The *Panzerkeil* (wedge) proved to be very successful, especially southwest of Kursk where the Soviet lines were penetrated and heavy losses inflicted on the defenders. The vehicles show dark green stripes painted over a dark yellow base, a camouflage scheme typical of mid-1943.

The crew members of this Pz.Kpfw. IV Ausf. G look rather worried as they cross a river. The front armor was reinforced to 80mm by welded-on plates, a change that was made on many reworked vehicles. The marking (a vertical bar over a horizontal bar) identifies the tank as part of 1.SS-Panzer-Division 'Leibstandarte Adolf Hitler'. Again, this was a temporary marking applied during the Battle of Kursk.

A late production Pz.Kpfw. III Ausf. L fitted with side skirts is being recovered by a Famo 18-ton half-track. The meaning of the black bars visible on the rear plate of the tank is unknown. It is probably a temporary unit marking used during Operation "Zitadelle".

This photograph shows a turretless Pz.Kpfw. III Ausf. J being used as an ammunition carrier. The crew is loading an MG34 into the vehicle. The tank is painted in a two-tone camouflage scheme, probably red brown over dark sand.

Many obsolete tanks were used by workshop units. The turret of this Pz.Kpfw. 38(t) was removed, then a crane was mounted on the engine cover. Note how the hull sinks while removing the engine cover of a damaged Pz.Kpfw. IV.

Guarding some supply lorries, a Pz.Kpfw. III Ausf. N passes by a destroyed T-34 Model 1943. With its side skirts and fenders still intact, the tank appears to be brand-new. The ubiquitous three-tone camouflage was applied to this tank, too.

Here a formation of late production or reworked Pz.Kpfw. IV Ausf. Gs of 2.SS-Panzer-Division is accompanied by a *Panzerbeobachtungswagen* (Pz.Beob.Wg.) III artillery observation vehicle. These specialized tanks were very similar to the command tanks, being fitted with extra radio and observation equipment. Note that tactical markings and the national insignia have been painted on the wooden box added on at the rear.

Here various elements of the German *Panzerwaffe* are represented as a section of armored personnel carriers accompanies the advance of Pz.Kpfw. III Ausf. L or M tanks. At the extreme right is visible a *Sturmflak*, a 2cm Flak 38 gun mounted on a 1-ton half-track.

An officer congratulates the commander of this PzKpfw. III Ausf. M after a successful combat. The tank, photographed near Mius in mid-1943, features a rack on the engine cover. The Pz.Kpfw. III tanks, with their 50mm armor and 5cm L/60 gun, were actually obsolete at this time.

A Pz.Kpfw. IV Ausf. H (an early one as indicated by the extra muffler to the left of the exhaust) undergoes repair work in the summer of 1943. The complete final drive, a common source of problems on German tanks, has been removed. The engine coolers are visible at the opened engine covers.

From mid-1943 onward, tank artillery units were sent to the front lines in greater numbers. This battery of 10.5cm le.FH 18/2 guns mounted on Gw. II Wespe vehicles prepares to support an attack with indirect fire. The obsolete Pz.Kpfw. IIs were used in a very sensible way, like their big brother the Hummel, and the Wespe performed well up to the end of the war.

Another stop-gap solution was the Marder II. The German 7.5cm Pak 40 was fitted onto the hull of the Pz.Kpfw. II, thus creating yet another tank hunter. This vehicle features a three-tone camouflage scheme applied with a brush. Close scrutiny of the photo will reveal the name of the driver's wife, Dorle, painted on the visor.

Moving through a corn field, this Marder III searches for targets. Due to the lack of capable tanks in 1942, many self-propelled guns were developed. This ex-Soviet 7.62cm gun was fitted onto the hull of the Pz.Kpfw. 38(t). Used in action in North Africa and in Russia, these tank hunters proved to be quite effective. Due to their inadequate armor protection, though, their service life was short.

Ready to unleash the deadly force of its 7.5cm Pak 40 gun, a perfectly camouflaged Marder II seeks cover in a ravine. Before the tank destroyer goes back into combat, some of the foliage used to hide it will be removed to give the gunner a clear view through his telescope.

A pair of Marder III Ausf. H maneuvers through a village. Based on the hull of the Pz.Kpfw. 38(t), this tank hunter used the German 7.5cm Pak 40. The lead vehicle is thoroughly camouflaged, while the second is finished in plain dark yellow. Living and fighting in these tiny vehicles was not easy, and the crew had no protection from the weather. Posing a danger to all Soviet tanks, these tank hunters had to rely on their speed and agility when changing position.

Supporting the advance of an APC section, a 3.7cm Flak 43 mounted on a 5-ton half-track waits for low-flying dive bombers. Combat tactics like this were hazardous for the half-track crews since they enjoyed no protection at all. Losses were very high in the *Sturmflak* units.

Officers of a *Panzergrenadier* unit interrogate Russian prisoners of war. The vehicle at left is a Sd.Kfz. 251/6 (Ausf. C), the one at right a Sd.Kfz. 250/3. Both vehicles were prime targets for enemy guns because they were easily recognizable from a distance as command vehicles due to their conspicuous frame antennas.

A mixed column of trucks carry supplies to the front. The mixture of types clearly shows the problems faced by the German armament industry. The lead vehicle is a 1.5-ton Phenomen Granit. The second and third are Opel Blitz 3000 A trucks, which are followed by a Maultier half-track.

One of the more rare vehicles used by the *Wehrmacht* was the Sd.Kfz. 251/17. Designed as an armored antiaircraft gun, this weapon mounted the 2cm Flak 38 in the cramped crew compartment of a medium APC. This vehicle did not prove to be practical, however. Side traverse was not sufficient, and limited elevation made engagement of ground targets impossible.

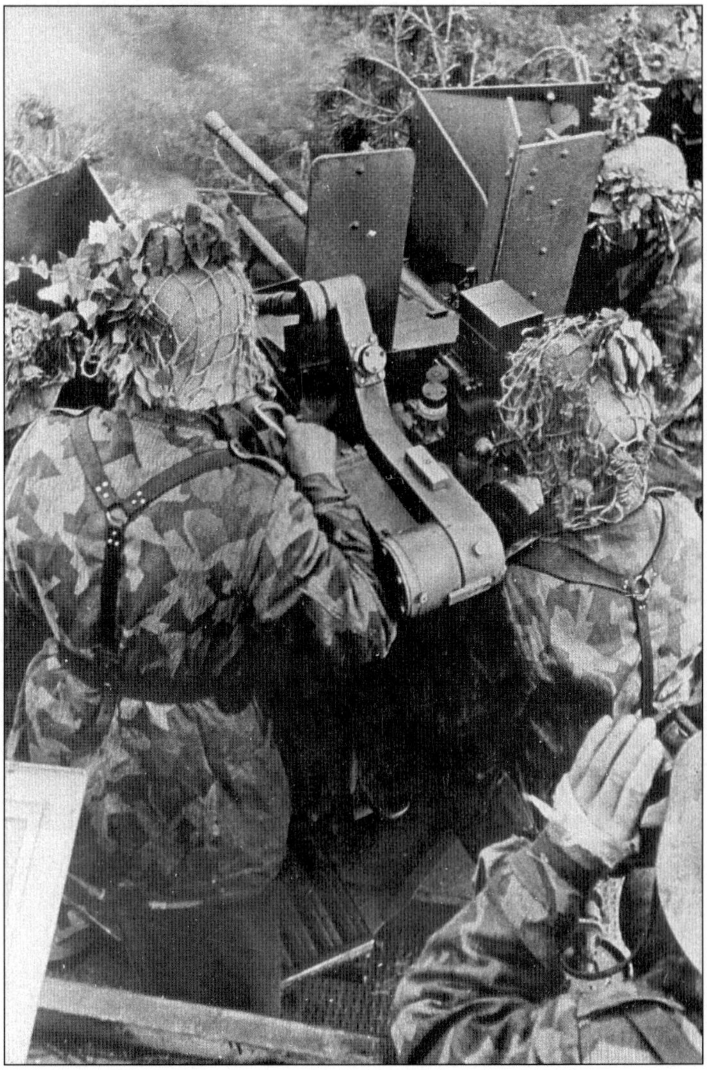

Engaging a ground target, this quadruple *Flakvierling* fires with all barrels. Offering a high rate of fire, these guns were very effective against soft targets. The loading of ammunition was complicated, however. Each gunner had to take care of two guns, changing the 20-round magazines every few minutes. This procedure was not easy as both gunners had to coordinate the exchange with the gunner.

Marder II (7.62cm Pak 36(r) auf Pz.Kpfw. II Ausf. D/E), unidentified unit, Stalingrad, winter 1942/43

This tank hunter is camouflaged with a scruffy winter whitewash over a dark gray base color (RAL 7021). Unlike one year earlier, the units at this time were supplied with appropriate equipment and paint. The vehicle displays a prominent German cross, but no further markings. With the spring coming, the first rains slowly but surely washed off the paint. With the addition of mud, the vehicles blended well with the surroundings.

Pz.Kpfw. III Ausf. L, 10.Panzer-Division, Tunisia, late 1942

Toward the end of hostilities in North Africa, the Germans used different camouflage colors. This Pz.Kpfw. III Ausf. L is finished in RAL 8020 desert yellow. Some units used a second color, RAL 7027 light brown, for camouflage. The only visible marking consists of a red '7', which denotes the company. The ubiquitious dust of the region would have covered the entire vehicle under a heavy layer of natural camouflage.

Pz.Kpfw. VI Ausf. E Tiger, s.Pz.Abt.501, Tunis, spring 1943

Some of the vehicles of s.Pz.Abt.501 were finished in an unofficial light olive green. This paint was probably chosen by the unit because the terrrain of Tunisia consisted more of green shades. The tank carries prominent tactical numbers on its turret, which made direction for the Abteilung commander easy. A camouflage net was used to further conceal the vehicle.

Pz.Kpfw. IV Ausf. F2, Pz.Rgt.36, 14.Panzer-Division, Russia, southern district, spring 1943

When new camouflage colors were introduced, the tank units would receive the paint to redo their vehicles. Although tanks were normally not overpainted near the front lines, some vehicles received irregular camouflage patterns applied with these paints. This Pz.Kpfw. IV is decorated with narrow lines of RAL 7028 dark yellow over a dark gray base color. The shape of the tank was effectively broken up by the paint scheme, and local mud or dust would further conceal the tank.

Pz.Kpfw. V Ausf. D, Pz.Abt.51, Kursk area, July 1943

All German tanks sent to the Eastern Front in the spring of 1943 were delivered in dark yellow (RAL 7028 or something similar). The units were provided with camouflage colors, and they then painted their tanks according to the surroundings. In this example, Pz.Abt.51 applied dark green stripes, which was the typical mid-1943 scheme. The turret number '045' denotes the tank as being a staff vehicle.

Pz.Kpfw. III Ausf. M, unidentified unit, Kursk area, summer 1943

Another fine example of a typical mid-1943 pattern, this Pz.Kpfw. III Ausf. M, which belongs to an unknown unit, is camouflaged with irregular narrow dark green stripes over a dark yellow base. Large German crosses have been painted on the hull side skirts. This tank was another staff vehicle of the II.Abteilung of the regiment. A Nazi flag is spread over the turret basket for air recognition.

Sd.Kfz. 251/17, Panzer-Division 'Hermann Göring', Sicily, summer 1943

This armored half-track is one of the few produced with its superstructure widened to accomodate the 2cm Flak 38 gun. The vehicle wears the 1943-pattern camouflage. In this case, the dark green stripes were painted rather than sprayed over the dark yellow base. The red number identifies the Sd.Kfz 251 as the eighth vehicle of its company.

Pz.Kpfw. IV Ausf. H, Pz.Rgt.29, 12.Panzer-Division, central Russia, autumn 1943

This Pz.Kpfw. IV Ausf. H is a fine example of how the 1943-pattern camouflage could be adapted to local conditions. In an area of lush vegetation, Pz.Rgt.29 increased the proportion of dark green, creating a spider's web of green stripes over the vehicle's dark yellow base. The vehicle features both the tactical number and division insignia painted on the turret skirts.

Pz.Kpfw. VI Ausf. E Tiger, s.Pz.Abt.502, Russia, late 1943

This Tiger of s.Pz.Abt.502 wears a camouflage scheme typical for the autumn, and for southern Russia's dry climate. Large brown blotches (RAL 8017) have been applied to the dark yellow base. Often enough, the vehicles were covered with mud to further help them blend in with the surroundings. Small turret numbers are visible painted in black. Note that the mudguards are missing.

StuG III Ausf. G, unknown StuG.Brig., southern Russia, spring 1944

Very similar to the Tiger above, this StuG III Ausf. G shows a brown (RAL 8017) camouflage scheme applied in broad lines over the dark yellow base. Relatively little remains of the base color. This mid- production StuG is fitted with the late-style Saukopf mantlet, and a large crate is located on the engine deck, which was typical for StuG units.

15cm s.FH 18 auf Gw III/IV Hummel, Pz.Art.Rgt.116, Russia, summer 1944

Painted in a standard summer camouflage scheme, this Hummel was finished with dark green stripes over dark yellow. The vehicle shows a full array of markings. The vehicle number and German cross were applied to the superstructure's sides. The tactical sign of the 3rd heavy battery, as well as the 5.Panzer-Division's symbol, were painted on the left front of the superstructure.

StuG III Ausf. G, StuG.Brig.245, France, summer 1944

This StuG of StuG.Brig.245 shows yet another two-tone camouflage scheme. The interesting pattern shows dark green (RAL 6003) applied in broad horizontal stripes. The brigade insignia, the German cross, and the vehicle number are all painted on the side skirts.

Pz.Kpfw. II Ausf. L Luchs, 116.Panzer-Division, France, summer 1944

This light reconnaissance vehicle is finished with small dark green blotches over a dark yellow base. The vehicle number '4121' was painted on the turret in black with white outline. These vehicles were very popular due to their high speed. They were occasionally called 'Mini-Panthers' by the US due to the similar running gear.

Pz.Kpfw. V Ausf. G Panther, unknown unit, Western Front, autumn 1944

This Panther shows the typical 1944 camouflage consisting of dark green and brown blotches over a dark yellow base. The proportion of the lighter dark yellow was decreased, making it more suitable for the temperate climate of middle Europe. German crosses and a low-visibility number were also applied. Typical for the Western Front, the vehicle is partially camouflaged with foliage.

Pz.Kpfw. VI Ausf. B Tiger, s.Pz.Abt. 'Feldherrnhalle', Hungary, early winter 1945

This early-production Tiger Ausf. B was completely whitewashed to blend with the snow. The vehicle, which is equipped with the early Porsche-style turret, is completely covered with Zimmerit. Besides the German cross and the nickname 'Anneliese', no further markings are evident.

Jagdtiger, s.Pz.Jäg.Abt.512, Germany, spring 1945

This ultra-heavy tank hunter, the Jagdtiger, is decorated in a non-standard camouflage pattern. Towards the end of the war, supply problems forced the tank troops to use whatever was available to camouflage their vehicles. In this case, the Jagdtiger was delivered wearing only a coat of rust red primer. A camouflage pattern of dark yellow and dark gray (RAL 7021) was then sprayed over this base.

This fine view shows infantrymen mounting a StuG III Ausf. G, which is fitted with side skirts and wooden beams. *Panzergrenadiers* often fought alongside assault gun units. Towards the end of the war, more and more assault guns were used primarily for tank destroying rather than infantry support.

A 4.5-ton lorry (possibly a Büssing) recovers a Demag 1-ton half-track that has slipped off the road. The truck carries a Bilstein crane, which was standard equipment for workshop units. Note that winter-weather chains have been applied to the rear tires. An earlier recovery attempt using a towing bar failed, so the crane was put into action.

A surviving Sd.Kfz. 252 supplies a StuG III Ausf. G in mid-1943. The low silhouette of the half-track allowed it to be concealed easily during combat. The assault gun carries three long wooden beams on each side for additional 'armor' protection. The national marking and vehicle number are painted on a thin piece of sheet metal attached to the beams. The hull sides have been reinforced by sections of spare tracks.

'Jaguar', a StuG III Ausf. G with extra bolted-on armor, has been moved into a garage. The assault gun is finished in plain dark yellow and displays its tactical sign on the left side of the nose plate. Assault gun units often gave names to vehicles, a practice that probably stemmed from the old German artillery tradition of denoting guns by letters.

In this dramatic photograph, an early production StuG III Ausf. G passes by a destroyed T-34 Model 1934. The Soviet tank apparently drove into a ditch, was spotted by the enemy and then subsequently blasted. The main problem of assault guns is evident here. Encountering the enemy in such a situation, the entire vehicle had to turn around on the narrow road. A tank would merely have to turn its turret.

The crew of this StuG III replenish ammunition under cover of a farmhouse. The Ausf. G normally carried 54 rounds, but experienced crews removed the storage racks, thus doubling the capacity. Assault gun crew members were considered the elite of the artillery branch, and they were even issued special uniforms.

The loader of a StuG III opens fire at Soviet infantry. To get a clear shot, he has affixed his MG34 to the holder originally intended for AA defence. Crouching behind a hatch, an infantryman seeks cover. This Ausf. G is from the one production lot fitted with smoke candles. Its camouflage consists of dark green stripes over a dark yellow base.

1943 was the year of the Tiger tank. Due to its heavy armor and deadly 8.8cm gun, it could easily destroy any enemy tank. The tank seen here, an early version, is painted in a three-tone camouflage pattern. Portions of the anti-magnetic *Zimmerit* are missing on the bow plate. Otherwise, the vehicle seems to be brand-new. The APCs in the background belong to Pz.Gren.Div. 'Großdeutschland'.

Two Tigers of s.Pz.Abt.501 meet after combat. The scarred and barren trees provide mute testimony of heavy fighting. Sometimes the tank crews could be careless, especially in wooded areas. Soviet snipers inflicted heavy losses on the Germans.

Railway transport was a common means of covering long distances during the war. Here a company of Tiger Ausf. E tanks is seen loaded for transport. Being too wide, the Tigers normally were fitted with a narrow transport track, but that was not done in this case, possibly due to time restraints. The vehicles are of different production lots, as is evident by the different commander's cupolas. Being produced after August 1943, only the second tank is covered with *Zimmerit* paste.

A long column of Panther tanks speeds down a seemingly endless stretch of road as it moves up to the front. When introduced in mid-1943, these tanks proved to be far from perfect. Some months later, however, the Panther became the best medium tank of World War Two.

This interesting photo shows a Panzerbefehlswagen III Ausf. K command tank. The star antenna is visible on the rear of the engine deck. The commander and the two other officers standing in the VW Schwimmwagen use binoculars to watch the battle from a distance.

This heavily retouched photo shows a well-equipped workshop behind the lines. The heavy Tiger tanks required specially designed equipment. To remove the turret, portal cranes were used. Note how the control cable is attached to the lugs on the side of the turret.

The crew of this reworked Pz.Kpfw. IV Ausf. G appears happy while posing for the camera. Perhaps this photo was taken after heavy fighting. The tank is packed tight with extra track links for maximum armor protection. The name 'Heidi' is just visible on the driver's visor.

Whenever possible, German armored units were transported via rail. Though the destination could be reached relatively quickly, train lines were prime targets for fighter-bombers. Here a train loaded with a Tiger and several StuG IIIs waits for shipment. The Tiger is rather battered, lacking two of its roadwheels.

This mid-production Tiger is transporting at least ten German soldiers, who are intrigued by a group of Soviet POWs. The photo was taken in the Ukraine during the turn of the year 1943/44. The fighting here inflicted heavy losses on both sides. During the winter the Germans lost about 1,700 tanks, and the Soviets more than 4,500.

This photo quite dramatically illustrates the superiority of the Tiger tank. Though a number of hits are evident, not one has penetrated the heavy armor. The damaged roadwheel appears to be somewhat perforated by artillery splinters, however. The crew of this early Tiger is reloading ammunition. Note that the empty cartridges from the previous battle have been thrown to the ground.

Once again infantrymen mount a StuG III for an easy ride to the front lines. Though comfortable, this practise could be dangerous since tanks tended to attract enemy attention. The standing trooper holds an MG42, while all the other troops are equipped with old-fashioned rifles. All of them wear the reversible white winter uniform. The StuG also sports appropriate winter camouflage.

Taking a ride on a tank, several *Panzergrenadier* (mechanized infantry) troops pose for a photo. This Pz.Kpfw. IV is an early Ausf. H, as is evident by the antenna (which was fitted to the left rear corner of the hull) and the additional armor plates.

In this impressive photo, the crew of an Sd.Kfz. 251 seek cover behind the decorated machine gun shield of their armored personnel carrier. Apart from an assortment of trucks, tanks and aircraft, eight landing crafts and a balloon were also destroyed by this unit.

The Year 1944

A column of Tigers moves through heavy mud. Their camouflage consists simply of a whitewash, which blends perfectly with the snow. Here, however, a thaw has begun on the Eastern Front. This meant that all movement became difficult, especially for wheeled vehicles and foot soldiers.

Two Pz.Kpfw. IVs take position behind a slope. Here the *Panzers* can easily open fire on approaching enemy tanks, who won't be able to spot more than their turrets. These Ausf. H or J variants are fitted with turret skirts only, with spare tracks being used to reinforce the hull armor. Note that the tank in the distance has a prominent hole in its turret skirt. This hit probably destroyed the turret basket, but apparently did not penetrate the armor.

A battery of StuG III Ausf. Gs prepares for action. All the vehicles have been modified by the addition of extra armor plates, probably made from surplus side skirts. Losses from snipers were high, but this remedy would offer at least some protection.

At least 20 infantrymen have taken the opportunity to hitch a comfortable ride on this StuG III Ausf. G. The StuG commander is barely visible, wearing the single black jacket among the white winter uniforms. Assault guns needed infantry support because their side traverse was dangerously limited.

A valuable support weapon, this 15cm *Nebelwerfer* rocket launcher mounted on a 2-ton Maultier moves steadily through the snow. Fully armored, this vehicle was very successful. The vehicle commander stands in his open hatch. Note the MG34 mounted for close combat defense.

Standing still in its tracks, this StuG III waits for further orders. This late Ausf. G, which is in mint condition, is possibly a new vehicle. Of note are the large sections of spare tracks that have been applied to the casemate's frontal slopes.

The Wespe's big brother was the Hummel (bumblebee). Armed with a 15cm s.FH 18, this self-propelled gun was a logical supplement to any Panzer artillery regiment. This photo shows a Hummel unit entraining prior to being shipped off to the front.

Photographed from behind, this Hummel is an ammunition transporter. In emergency situations, it could be easily transformed into a gun carrier. Its camouflage consists of brown blotches with green outlines on dark yellow ground. The Pz.Kpfw. III seen at the left probably is an artillery observer's vehicle.

Maintaining a steady supply of fuel was a constant problem for the German troops. The decision to use Otto engines instead of the more economical diesel helped to worsen the situation. Here a 200-liter fuel barrel is being loaded aboard a Nashorn tank hunter. The vehicle shows a scruffy camouflage and some additional foliage.

Advancing slowly after a (successful?) attack, this StuG III is followed by two soldiers who warily search for targets. The commander and gunner peep out of their hatches very carefully, hoping to avoid incurring the head injuries that were so common among tankers. The assault gun is provided with a frame around the engine deck to carry additional equipment.

A Panther Ausf. G slowly advances through a corn field with the support of lightly equipped infantry. The Panther, which is not painted in any camouflage scheme, wears the tactical marking 'IN3'. This identifies the tank as a staff vehicle.

This photo shows a vehicle from the same unit (this time an Ausf. A) speeding up. The infantrymen have to run to keep up with it, which is no easy job loaded down with equipment and weapons. One single track link was placed upon the engine cover, which is unusual. The Panther's *Zimmerit* coating is visible on the turret.

Destroyed and abandoned, this Panther Ausf. G stands as a witness to the rigors of combat in the East. Although no hit is visible, the vehicle seems to have been burned out. With the torsion bars melted, the tank has sunk to the ground, giving it an almost deflated appearance.

Two more unfortunate Panthers from the same unit. Possibly an entire unit was caught by surprise by an air raid. The Soviet Stormovik diver bombers were highly feared enemies. The shells spread around on the ground indicate that the tanks were looted .

A moment of triumph! The crew of a StuG III Ausf. G inspects its victim — a T-34 Model 1943. The assault gun has small mottles of dark green and brown applied to its side skirts, which is certainly not a particularly good camouflage scheme. Apart from the German cross national insignia painted on the side skirts, no further markings are visible.

This photo shows a battery of StuG III Ausf. Gs with their guns elevated. The camouflage scheme they wear is interesting and effective, successfully breaking up the shape of the vehicle. Heavy foliage was also attached to the assault guns, which is probably the best camouflage of all.

Another StuG III Ausf. G, this one fitted with smoke candles, somewhere in the vast and empty plains of Russia. This vehicle is also effectively camouflaged. The additional armor on this assault gun has been welded rather than bolted on.

Very effectively concealed indeed, this StuG III awaits the enemy at a farmyard. The front of the assault gun is covered by large straw mats, leaving only a slit for the gun. The gunner is incapable of seeing anything, so this must be merely a propaganda shot.

Here the formerly hidden StuG III is visible. Note that the slopes over the driver are reinforced by concrete and the muzzle brake is covered with a protective bag. The vehicle also features a Saukopf mantlet and massive 80mm armor. Both towing ropes are mounted.

A StuG III belonging to StuG.-Brig.245 prepares for street fighting. The vehicle is interesting due to the horizontally applied camouflage scheme and the unit insignia, which was painted on the side skirts. The gun and superstructure are protected against bad weather by a large tarpaulin.

Increasing losses during ground combat led to production of semi-armored half-tracks. At least the driver and co-driver were protected to a certain degree. The gun crew, however, still sat in the rain. This Sd.Kfz. 7/2 carried the very successful 3.7cm Flak gun.

This Sd.Kfz. 251 APC, which is being inspected by Generalfeldmarshall von Rundstedt, is very interesting. A command vehicle from an artillery unit, it is equipped with a search light and has a persicope fitted at the co-driver's position. The half-track is painted with a camouflage scheme of dark yellow stripes over a dark green base.

Introduced in 1943, the *Wespe* (wasp) self-propelled gun significantly improved the mobility and effectiveness of German field artillery. The gun in the foreground has just fired a round, and its 10.5cm barrel is seen at full recoil. Note that all personal belongings of the crew are stowed outside; the cramped interior did not leave any space for non-essential items.

A battery of Hummel SP guns in action. The lack of defensive preparations indicates that this gun position was established in a hurry. The distance between the guns is pretty close, so the battery must not expect to be menaced by air strikes or enemy ground forces.

Introduced two years previously, many of these Marder III tank hunters were still in combat in 1944. Built on a proven and reliable chassis, the Pz.Kpfw. 38(t), these fast and agile vehicles were able to stop Soviet tank attacks. Due to weak armor protection, however, losses were high in the *Panzerjäger* units.

Moving slowly through a blossoming field, this Tiger Ausf. E is followed by a squad of paratroopers. The Tiger shows an elaborate camouflage scheme of dark green and brown stripes over a dark yellow base. The vehicle number is not painted on the turret basket, but rather to the left of it. The s.Pz.Abt.502 fought in the northern sector in defense of East Prussia.

Late-production Marder IIIs wait in a row on a street in Flanders while awaiting a call to action. The vehicles are brand-new and show no added camouflage scheme. The guns, however, which were delivered from other firms, show the typical 1944 finish. It is very likely that the SP guns will be camouflaged soon. Though more popular than the earlier Ausf. H, the Ausf. M also suffered from its thin armor. Besides from direct gun fire, artillery bombardments were most dangerous.

One of the weirder vehicles used by the *Wehrmacht* was this 7.5cm Pak 40 auf GW Lorraine Schlepper(f). Due to the limited supply of tanks, many SP guns were improvised on captured enemy equipment. Shortages of spare parts, an excessive overload of the chassis and the very limited interior restricted the combat value of these weapons.

Heading up to the front, the crew of this Marder III Ausf. M finds it more desirable to ride atop the tiny vehicle rather than travel inside of it. Large amounts of ammunition and fuel were carried within the vehicle. The muzzle brake cover reveals a cat's eye.

It is almost impossible to say what vehicle is concealed behind this mass of foliage. However, the driver's vision slit is visible below the gun, indicating that this is a Sd.Kfz. 7/1 with 2cm Flakvierling. The gun crew commander is scanning the sky with his binoculars for a likely target.

The crew of this Jagdpanzer IV (7.5cm L/48) of *Panzerlehrdivision* enjoys a meal on top of their vehicle. The spare track links fitted to the rear indicate that this is a late production tank hunter. *Zimmerit* is once again visible on all armor plates.

Photographed while passing tank obstacles somewhere in Italy, this StuG III Ausf. G demostrates the usefulness of static lines of defense in mobile warfare. Like all fortifications before, the *Gotenlinie* in Italy, and later the *Westwall* or Siegfried Line in France, were demolished by air raids and artillery fire and outflanked by amored formations.

Lieutenant Ludwig discusses the situation in front of his assault gun. The officer from StuG.Brig.346 was awarded the Iron Cross for destroying 16 British tanks in just a few minutes of combat. The barrel of his StuG III is decorated with 17 rings.

This Panther was destroyed by Polish troops during the fighting in the Falaise pocket in August. This bloody combat inflicted heavy losses on both sides. This Ausf. A wears a very uneven *Zimmerit* coating. Note the extensive damage to the left fender.

This Pz.Kpfw. IV Ausf. G (reworked) suffered a remarkable fate: the barrel of its 7.5cm L/43 gun was penetrated by a well-placed shot. Having immediately withdrawn itself from combat, the vehicle was saved and repaired. The Pz.Kpfw. IV shows retrofitted additional armor welded to the front and side skirts. The antenna, however, is still mounted on the right side of the hull.

An artillery battery assembles on a road in France in the autumn of 1944. Due to the Allied air supremacy, all movement during daylight was hazardous. In fact, the Germans lost a high proportion of their reinforcements while they were en route to the front. The lead vehicle is a late-production Sd.Kfz. 7 with a wooden body. It tows the barrel of a 15cm Kanone 18, a heavy gun that was carried in two loads.

Another late-model 8-ton half-track tows a 15cm s.FH 18. The gun is partially concealed with heavy foliage. The barrel is moved back on the carriage for long range transports. This gun was the backbone of German artillery.

The effect of massive air strikes is evident in this dramatic photo. A Pz.Kpfw. IV was completely destroyed by a direct hit, and two Sd.Kfz. 251 were damaged or overturned by the impact of the shells. The overturned half-track probably carried a 2cm Flak 38, as is evident by the broken barrel.

A fine view of a late-production Pz.Kpfw. Ausf. J. The tank was hit at the turret edge, but probably some other rounds penetrated its armor and caused a fire. All rubber coatings have burned down to ash. The G.I. is holding on to a wire mesh screen known as a *Thoma Schild* (Thoma shield), which was an antibazooka shield.

This Pz.Kpfw. IV, which was captured intact by US troops, is being moved back to the rear for evaluation. Although obsolete, the Pz.Kpfw. IV, with its 7.5cm L/48 gun, was able to knock out any Allied tank at normal combat ranges.

These two *Raupenschlepper Ost* (RSO) tracked vehicles were pressed into service by US troops. Intended for the rough conditions of the Eastern Front, it was a slow mover with a maximum speed of 15-20 km/h (9-12 mph). However, its cross-country mobility was legendary. A large American flag is displayed to protect the Americans on board from a fatal case of mistaken identity.

A Tiger tank passes by a column of Pz.Kpfw. IIIs and IVs in late 1944. All of the tanks show a scruffy winter whitewash. The Pz.Kpfw. IV Ausf. H to the left carries a number of spare tracks as additional armor protection. The introduction of the JS (Joseph Stalin) heavy tank and the T-34/85 posed a great threat to the more lightly armored German tanks.

Another Tiger of s.Pz.Abt. 502 prepares for action against the Soviets in an East Prussian town in late 1944. A number of paras have mounted the tank. The s.Panzer-Abteilung 502 was able to destroy large numbers of tanks, but the Soviets were able to compensate for their losses. Note that even the heavily armored Tigers used extra track links for increased protection.

Always the last hope, an 8.8cm Flak 36 gun secures an important supply road. The antiaircraft gun is perfectly camouflaged in winter-white paint, while the Ford Maultier half-track passing at left still wears its summer paint scheme.

This 8.8cm Pak 43 has been effectively dug-in in expectation of a tank attack. The soldier to the right employs a range finder to make long range shots more accurate. There are cases known where such AT guns destroyed enemy tanks at distances well beyond 3,000m (3028 yards).

Captured during the first lucky days of the Ardennes offensive, these M-10 tank destroyers are put into action against the US troops. The inadequate supply of fuel and ammunition limited the use of captured equipment to only a few days.

The Year 1945

Expecting the Allied advance at Aachen in early 1945, this Panzer IV/70 (A) was thoroughly camouflaged by barn doors and sheets of wood. These vehicles, sometimes referred to as *Zwischenlösung* (interim solution), carried the same deadly 7.5cm KwK as the Panther MBT. The penetration data were similar to that of the 8.8cm, making these vehicles effective tank hunters.

Hidden behind houses in Aachen, the crew of a 3.7cm Flak 43 *Möbelwagen* waits for new orders. The street fighting here was dogged, so it is likely that this AA tank was involved in ground combat. The German *Flakpanzer* antiaircraft tanks were developed with limited means by Ostbau in Sagan. The results, however, were impressive.

The heaviest German tank in action was the Tiger Ausf. B. Weighing 70 tons, it combined heavy armor with the famous 8.8cm gun. Here crew members pose in front of a late production vehicle. It shows no *Zimmerit* coating and is finished in the 'ambush' scheme. (Photo: Gruber).

The engine of another Tiger Ausf. B is being replaced with the help of a Bilstein crane mounted on a Büssing NAG 4.5-ton lorry. The Tiger is fitted with narrow transport tracks, which were used during rail transport. (Photo: Gruber).

This Pz.Kpfw. IV Ausf. H was probably destroyed by an air raid. Many parts of the equipment are damaged, the right track being completely thrown off. Once immobilized, the tank was abandoned. A US 2.5-ton truck is passing on the road in the background.

A late-production StuG III Ausf. G anticipates a Soviet advance. Though it was an effective tank destroyer, there were never enough to stop the masses of Soviet tanks. This vehicle carries a lot of additional equipment and a fuel barrel. The armor shield of the remote-control MG is barely visible.

Rather battered, this StuG IV positions itself behind a 10.5cm le.FH 18/40. By the time this photo was taken, there were only isolated battle groups fielding a few tanks or assault guns. The times of large-scale operations were gone. The remaining *Panzers* were pitted against the victorious Soviets.

Destroyed by an adversary of equal ability, this Panther Ausf. G litters the road of Poznan, Poland. Two 122mm rounds from a JS-2 penetrated the 80mm frontal armor. Luckily, the crew of this tank had a chance to escape, since the transmission blocked the round.

Although the *Panzerwaffe* suffered only a fraction of Soviet losses, the number of German tanks decreased dramatically in late 1944. Here an abandoned Tiger Ausf. E lies in a ditch. As no damage is visible, this tank might have been left behind due to some minor problem like a shortage of fuel. This Tiger Ausf. E is a late-production vehicle with steel-rimmed running wheels and rotating commander's hatch.

This most interesting StuG III Ausf. G is probably one of those vehicles intended to be delivered to Finland. The armor cover over the driver's visor is a characteristic feature of these assault guns. The StuG was caught by artillery fire in Königsberg. The side skirts were modifications by a field workshop, since the original mounting proving to be too unstable.

Littering the same road, this StuG IV apparently lost its idler wheel. The damaged running gear stopped the vehicle, which had to be abandoned. Note that the MG shield of a Sd.Kfz. 251 was used to improve protection of the loader. Remnants of a three-tone camouflage are evident. The ammunition, more than 50 rounds, has already been recovered from the vehicle.

A lot of short-barrelled assault guns were still in service in 1945. This early-production StuG III Ausf. D was abandoned in Prague in May of 1945. After introduction of better ammunition for these guns in 1943, the combat value was increased again. However, combat against heavy tanks like the JS was senseless.

Sporting a very interesting camouflage of dark green or brown mottling over dark yellow, this late StuG III Ausf. G is seen in an eastern German town. Due to battle damage, the side skirts are missing and the rails were removed. Spare tracks were added to the superstructure's side as extra armor.

Passing a 1945 vintage German supply convoy, a Panther Ausf. G speeds ahead. The tank is equipped with a wooden pole for recovery purposes. The Panther is often referred to as the best medium tank of WWII. It was indeed a perfect symbiosis of mobility, firepower and armor protection.

A section of Sd.Kfz. 251/7 *Pioniergruppenwagen* (engineer vehicles) waits in a traffic jam near Lake Balaton on a wet, gloomy day in early 1945. The powerful Hanomag was a reliable vehicle, but there were never enough of them.

Three Sd.Kfz. 250 light APCs sit deserted in a town somewhere in eastern Germany. All three vehicles are painted in plain dark yellow with no camouflage scheme being evident. Apart from the comparatively large German crosses, no further tactical markings are evident.

This Sd.Kfz. 7/2, which is fitted with an armored cabin, was abandoned after an unsuccessful attempt to repair the front axle. In the background, the ruins of a German city testify that the the end of the war is fast approaching.

This late production Pz.Kpfw. IV Ausf. J, which is fitted with wire-mesh *Thoma* shields, was destroyed somewhere in Poland. The turret was penetrated by a clean hit, possibly by 85mm fire. Note that the Bosch headlight was turned to the back in order to protect the glass.

A vehicle dump in Kurland, shortly after the end of hostilities. A number of BA 10s are visible in the long row of vehicles. These armored cars, captured 4 years earlier, were used in an anti-partisan role. A more sophisticated ex-French Panhard armored car was pressed into service for the same purpose.

The war is over! Two ancient armored cars stand in the shadow of the *Reichskansleri* (the Chancellory) as symbols of the last-ditch effort and utter defeat of the German defenders. The vehicle in the foreground is a *Schupo-Sonderwagen* (police armored car) produced under the restrictions of the Treaty of Versailles in the early 1920s. The weird vehicle in the background is an armored car based on a Krupp Protze, which was produced for Dutch-India in the early 1930s.

Life goes on, even after a lost war. German farm wives harvest potatoes beside a destroyed Panther Ausf. G. The length of the 7.5cm L/70 gun is well illustrated here. The high-velocity gun was one of the most powerful during this period. It was used by the French after the war in a number of light tanks and armored cars.